MW01068453

A Bite-Sized Business Book

Contract Management for Non-Specialists

Paul Davies

Copyright Paul Davies 2014

ISBN: 9781521102763

Published by:

Bite-Sized Books Ltd
Cleeve Croft, Cleeve Road, Goring RG8 9BJ UK
information@bite-sizedbooks.com
Registered in the UK. Company Registration No: 9395379

Contents

Chapter 1

Introduction

Chapter 2

Your Objectives as a Contract Manager

Chapter 3

Conventions

Chapter 4

Reading a Contract

Chapter 5

Contracts

Chapter 6

Managing the Contract

Chapter 7

Active Reading Summary

Chapter 8

The Successful Contract Manager

Chapter 9

Reassurance

Chapter 10

Next Steps

Chapter 11

Conclusion

Bite-Sized Books

Chapter 1

Introduction

There is a world of difference between contract management and successful contract management – and this book is dedicated to ensuring that you are successful in your contract management. That doesn't mean that you will never have any contractual disputes, that there won't be flash points and there will be no misunderstandings or breakdowns in communication – though this book will help you minimise them – but one clear aim of this book is to ensure that the project or programme that is the subject of the contract is delivered properly and effectively. For me that is the mark of a successful contract manager – although you will find examples, as I have, where somehow the contract becomes more important than achieving the aims of the contract.

This book, *Contract Management for Non-Specialists,* is aimed at business managers, project managers and sales people who are engaged with clients delivering services and products within a contractual framework. It is not designed to replace legal advice from qualified practitioners but will enable you to find your way round a contract, understand legal terms or find out what they mean, and allow you to have confidence in managing a contract either with a supplier or on behalf of a supplier.

This book and the role of the contract manager therefore isn't about dispute resolution, but about dispute prevention or, at least, mitigation. Disputes will arise in any sale of products and services and knowing where they are likely to occur, and how to defuse them rather than eventually resolve them will be crucial.

It's good practice to ensure that nothing you do can be construed as in any way fraudulent or an attempt to get round your legal obligations. This may seem common sense, and it is, but if you think that any step is questionable, it both probably is and you should take legal advice.

Contract law differs in different jurisdictions and the two major law systems, common law and civil law (three if you include Islamic), have quite different processes and approaches. With all the differences, there are still common elements because a contract in any system is there to define what is going to be delivered, how it is going to be delivered, and what will happen when the unexpected – which, of course should always be expected – occurs.

Essentially a contract is best seen as buying a promise and it details what one side will provide, under what conditions and in what circumstances, in return for a consideration, usually financial, of some sort from the other side. While not always strictly needed, it is always advisable in a business setting to have a contract in writing which is then signed by both parties Generally money changes hands, but the timing of that monetary exchange and under what conditions it will happen is usually made explicit in the contract and that is the type of business issue that we are concerned with here.

It is best to think of a contract as a worst case scenario. If you could just buy something, pass the money over, receive a receipt, and when you tried to use what you had bought found that it functioned perfectly, that it had been delivered on time and in good condition, and you could guarantee that that would happen every time, you would hardly need a contract. But suppliers run out of their raw materials and cannot manufacture in time, people who should provide a service go off sick or resign, wars break out and disrupt deliveries, and customers go bankrupt, refuse to pay, or promise to pay and then do may do nothing.

A contract won't prevent any of those unpleasant events, but a contract is what binds the parties to do something, and then both can sue and be sued as a worse case on that promise if anything goes wrong.

This **Bite-Sized Business Book** comes into play after the contract has been developed, argued over, then signed, and just before the project proper starts and then continues throughout the life of the contract. Ideally the person managing the contract should have been involved at an earlier stage but it is not essential and not that common in practice. It is usually possible for the contract manager to talk to the people who sold or bought the products or services before the contract is implemented and one assumption behind this book is that has happened and the contract manager has therefore a reasonable idea of what is to be delivered and on what terms even before reading the contract.

As any lawyer will tell you, going to court should be the last resort of a desperate person and not the first response. Courts are expensive, slow, sometimes unpredictable, sometimes capricious or appear to be to the lay person, and will sometimes cause more damage than immediate good. Legal action will tie up senior management time, cause endless internal angst and while easy to start prove quite impossible to stop. It is probably not even a good idea to threaten legal action let alone embark on it, though it may well become necessary.

Any sane contract manager will therefore look on his or her job as resolving any disputes as early as possible – perhaps anticipating them and stopping them before they start.

If the best sales opportunities are built (or at least cemented) on relationships, the fastest way to destroy that relationship once the project gets under way is to mention the contract. If you have to mention the contractual terms, you are already somewhere into a dispute. On the other hand, as the contract manager you will have to know the contract inside out. This book helps you with that apparent paradox.

Chapter 2

Your Objectives as a Contract Manager

The objectives of contract management and the contract manager are to:

- Understand the potential flash points in a contract before it starts to be implemented
- Understand the potential pinch points in the contract, such as critical delivery windows, and what contingency there might be
- Carefully focus on what the contract considers vital – it might be timeliness or quality or it might be both, for example, and can change during the life of the contract if agreed
- Understand any clauses that appear to you to be unequal in the contract and consider what effect they might have when managing the contract
- Monitor every stage of delivery
- Ensure that the bureaucratic structures – for example measurements of service level agreements (SLAs) – and other mechanisms, such as payments are all in place and work effectively
- Have a good grasp of what the acceptance criteria are and what issues they might cause
- Monitor every stage in the payment process
- Anticipate what risks exist and what issues might arise
- Have in place mitigating actions of various sorts
- Hold regular meetings with the opposite number in order to see what is happening from both sides.

As a good contract manager, you will obviously work out the points above from your own company's perspective. A brilliant contract manager will work out those points from both sides' point of view.

In practice you can boil this down to creating a good relationship with the contract manager on the other side. Between you, you should be able to work out as many worst case scenarios as there might be, understand what can be done to eliminate or mitigate those scenarios, and prevent any explosions on either side. And if it still goes thermo-nuclear, you will probably have prevented something much worse, if that is imaginable.

Chapter 3

Conventions

Take great note of the numbering system in contracts – an obvious point but sometimes people do not quite realise how carefully clauses in contracts are numbered. It is part of the internal reference system within a document – see below where the implications of this are explained – and really crucial. The major headings will have a single number, such as "2. Interpretation" then each sub-division of the clause will be numbered, using a variety of signifiers, so the first definition might appear as any of the following:

- 2.1 Definitions
- 2.a Definitions
- 2.i Definitions
- And so on.

Also note that in the preparation of a document it will have gone through many edits and changes and it is very common for versions of the contract to be known as *red-lined* or *clean*. Red-lined refers to the version that is being marked up; clean is the latest version where all edits have been accepted or removed. It is not uncommon to find that in this process various remains of previous versions – almost like fossils – get left in or cause grammatical issues, for example references to clause numbers that are now wrong. It sometimes makes reading contracts awkward, but should not detain you much and you should just use your brain, which is what a court would expect you to do.

If any word is highlighted, and appears in, for example, **bold**, but it might be denoted in *italics*, this word is used in the way it was defined usually at the beginning of the document. For example, **Payment Date** is very specific and it relies precisely on the definition that has already been given, as we explain below.

Chapter 4
Reading a Contract

You understand the general purpose of a contract and the fact that it is usually straightforward except that it has to take into account as many worst cases as it can. As it is impossible to foresee everything that could go wrong, there are usually some catch-all clauses. Just because the particular issue over which a dispute has arisen has not been specifically mentioned in the contract, it is unlikely that it won't be catered for somehow.

Reading the contract sounds obvious, but people do find it difficult to find their way around a contract at first and they also tend to read contracts as though they are purely sequential, like a novel. You will see that it is just about possible to do that, but for most people it is necessary to follow through the various references.

The internal references within a contract can be tricky to deal with. For example you may come across text that says, "Except as stated in Clause 4.1 and Clauses 4.2.1 and 4.2.2 . . ." At that point it is usually important that you go to the clauses identified as exceptions and read them as an integral part of the clause you are currently reading because otherwise you will not have a full grasp. The complication is that you might find that Clause 4.2.2 refers to another clause, " ... except as stated in clauses 5.1 and 7.1", so you are now two levels deep in the contract and it can get worse. (There is a suspicion sometimes that this sort of complexity has another purpose. But that is to be cynical.)

Contracts are largely made up of two different types of text. The first is what lawyers call *boilerplate*, that is standard text that can apply to almost any contract and which can be cut and pasted into a contract, usually without much thought. Payment terms and statements about which jurisdiction applies are typical examples of boilerplate. The second type of contract wording is usually based on some initial boilerplate clauses which have been specially re-written for the specific purpose of an individual contract.

Always read and check what is apparently boilerplate text – it can be subtly altered and may cause you issues.

You will find that contracts aren't actually that difficult to read, at a basic literacy level. There are technical words sprinkled in them, like breach, but you can look them up in any reasonable dictionary and they rarely hold any terrors. A breach is, for example, where one party has done something that goes against the contractual terms.

The trouble with reading a contract is that while they are usually in relatively straightforward English or national language, they are often quite ambiguous. You will find that there are at least fifty shades of grey in most contracts, although it is unlikely that they will be even as gripping as the novel of that name. The biggest thing to guard against when reading a contract is allowing your mind to wander because it inevitably will. Read in bursts and don't try to absorb the whole thing at one sitting.

When you first open a contract, do check that the bureaucratic elements are right. Make sure that your company is specifically named, that the other party is specifically named, and that the version of the contract you have is the signed one. As there will be many versions it is easy to get the wrong one. The signatures will usually not be at the very end of the document, as several types of document will follow, for example schedules, warranties, statements of work, and other factual information. In some jurisdictions also check that every page is initialled by both parties, though this is by no means a universal requirement, as an additional check that you are working to the right contract.

It is very rare for there to be any difficulties over these matters, but it is more than likely that the document in front of you will have been through a series of drafting and re-drafting processes before it reached its final state and errors do creep in as we have suggested earlier.

Finally check that the subject of the contract is what you anticipate. It has been known for a similar but wrong contract to be used for the wrong project.

Starting Point

The next step is counter-intuitive but really very useful. Search for and read the clauses relating to the termination of the contract.

There are a number of reasons for this, not least to check that there is such a clause or series of clauses relating to termination. (It is not unknown for such a clause to be left out, bizarre though that is, and such an omission can cause enormous problems and ever larger legal bills.)

Termination clauses can be of two main types: *termination at will* and *termination for cause*. Termination can be after a fixed term, but that needn't concern us here.

Termination at will can be important, as it usually exposes companies to risk, and this will be covered later. Termination at will means that by giving a certain amount of notice, one or both parties, and sometimes it is just one of the parties, can terminate the contract without any particular reason. This is useful where there hasn't been any fundamental breach of the contract but so many niggly issues that keeping it going is more expensive than closing it down.

What is more important here is the termination for cause clause. The second and more important reason for addressing the termination clauses as early as this is that this part of the contract will tell you probably far more clearly than anything else what is the most significant element in the contract.

There will usually be some boilerplate in any termination for cause clauses, relating to disputes, non-delivery, or failure to perform. There will almost certainly also be some specific clauses, often relating to matters like product quality, acceptance criteria, regulations, conduct of individuals, timeliness, or payments, which should alert you to what was in the mind of the people, often on the other side, when they were drafting and agreeing the contract.

It is good practice to take real account of these clauses and any specific issues that they raise. If your company insisted on them being in the contract, it is often useful to know what was in the mind of your senior management at the time it was agreed. When you took on the contract management these particular insights might have been overlooked. If the other side insisted on these issues being specifically mentioned, you will be forewarned and forearmed about some of the really tricky flash points in the project.

Active Reading

In addition, contracts need to be read in an active way. It is very easy to read the documents and let them roll over you and find that you have reached the end of a clause and not really absorbed the content. Active reading in this sense is making sure that you are alert for triggers that should cause you to take stock. It is really important to make good notes about these issues, whether they are raised in the termination clause or elsewhere.

The following are examples of triggers or alerts that should make you sit up other than the formal delivery dates, acceptance criteria and payment schedules, but there are more:

- *. . within 30 days . .*
- *. . served in writing only to the address . .*

- .. *all of the seller's rights* ..
- .. *if any of the assets* ..
- .. *at completion the seller shall comply with its obligations set out in clause 3* ..

You will see the type of trigger we mean from these examples, and they generally are either very precise, giving a time limit for example, or all encompassing, creating or extending the limits of the contract. Every time you come across one of these triggers, make a note, because it may have implications for you when you are managing the contract.

In your active reading also take note of apparently harmless or general statements, as these generally have a specific meaning. If the contract states, .. *as a going concern* .. even though it is not highlighted, this will have a precise meaning.

Another common example is around the phrase, *best endeavours*. Relatively recently there has been case law which apparently does mitigate the precise meaning, but it is as well to be alive to its usual implications. *Best* here can be held to mean that all the resources of the company will have to be channelled into, for example, remedying the issue under dispute. Most contracts will substitute the word *reasonable*, but any adjective stated as a superlative, for example, *greatest*, *closest*, *most significant*, should be an alert or trigger to you when you are reading the contract. It will have implications beyond the casual meaning you might assume.

As indicated above, there may also be false references, that is references to clauses that have later been removed from the document in the drafting and redrafting process. Make a note of these too.

As contract manager you cannot assume that the drafting of the contract will have produced a document that you can work easily with.

With those preliminaries taken care of, it's time to start to absorb and understand the whole contract, and there is no substitute for a usually laborious read through.

Chapter 5
Contracts

Contracts will consist of a series of elements, which can include more than the following which is not an exhaustive list:

- A title page
- The main body of the contract
- The signing page
- Schedules relating to the contract, such as milestones and names of specific people associated with the contract
- Inventories of equipment and other lists
- Warranties and indemnities
- Disclosures
- Statements of work.

In the main body of the contract, there will generally be a selection of the following headings, although there may well be synonyms, and probably other headings as well:

- Purpose
- Interpretation and, or definitions
- Consideration or payments
- Acceptance
- Warranties and indemnities
- Warranty and support
- Risk
- Apportionments, prepayments and pupil number reimbursement
- Liabilities of the Supplier and the Customer
- Value Added Tax
- Third Party Supplier Contracts
- Data protection
- Guarantee, Indemnity and Security
- Confidentiality and announcements
- Further assurance
- Assignment

- Termination
- Whole agreement
- Variation
- Costs
- Notice
- Interest on late payment
- Severance
- Agreement survives completion
- Third party rights
- Assignment
- Arbitration
- Conflicting provisions
- Successors
- Counterparts
- Limitation of liability
- Regulatory issues
- Force Majeure
- Governing law and jurisdiction.

This rather daunting list – and there can be more – is actually less of an obstacle than it might seem, but, it should be stressed, there is no substitute for reading the whole document as soon as you can.

Your role is not to negotiate these but to understand them and interpret them so you can either deliver the products and services or receive the products and services, and in both cases process the payments. You will, however, form opinions about the sanity and wisdom of those people who drew up the contract and signed it, and before too long you should share your understanding, properly edited and sanitised, with those responsible so that they can avoid some of the issues they have caused.

Most of the headings are self-explanatory, and only the most significant are covered here in any detail, leaving the boilerplate for you to read and just check you understand.

Each of the headings is looked at next.

Interpretation

This will generally be all the definitions of the highlighted words in the contract and because they will have a special meaning, you have to know what those special or precise meanings are. For example, there might be a definition of Insolvency Event, which will have implications for the whole contract, perhaps leading to its termination. These are not difficult to understand but do need to be read actively looking for alerts and triggers. The definition of Insolvency Event, for example, might be drawn so wide that there is quite a risk to the delivery of the service, and, depending upon the conditions attached to the Insolvency Event, it might be a way for the supplier to terminate the contract at minimal cost. (Depending upon whether you are the supplier or the customer, this might have different implications.)

Following the definition of all the highlighted words will generally be some further general statements in sub-clauses, for example this type of common sense statement: " . . except where the context precludes, references to one gender should be read to include any other."

Acceptance

This clause is vital to the contract manager because it will define what constitutes acceptance of a delivery of a product or the recognition that a service has been provided and completed. Revenue recognition will generally depend upon the acceptance criteria for the supplier and so it is essential that you understand it and any triggers it may contain. For example it may say that all of a particular contractual obligation will have to be completely delivered and accepted formally before an invoice for that work may be raised. There will be a proviso that such acceptance will not be unreasonably delayed, but there can be a huge disparity between what one side considers unreasonable and what the other side does.

Whichever side of the divide you are on, this will be one of the areas that may take a great deal of your contract management time.

Warranties and indemnities

Nearly all contracts require warranties, that is statements which say that the other side can rely on what you have told them about specific issues and where there is, for example, ambiguity, a warranty will ensure that the other side does not lose out. These are battle grounds when contracts are being negotiated and buyers will want as many as possible and suppliers will want to provide as few as possible.

If there are any you do not understand when you read them, this initial reading of the contract is the time to raise the points and get clear definitions.

Indemnities are hostages to fortune and suppliers in general will avoid giving indemnities, which basically say that if things go wrong, this is how the customer will be recompensed, either in money, goods or extra services. Rarely but not without precedent the indemnity can work the other way round, so a customer can be at fault for not providing timely forecasts of demand, where that is a contractual obligation.

The clear issue that indemnities are focused on is consequent loss and both trying to avoid the supplier being responsible for the customer's consequent loss, and ensuring that the buyer is responsible. It may be that you as the customer are relying on a product being delivered to you by in a certain condition and if that does not happen you may lose far more than the immediate work that you are shipping to a third party. If, for example, some contamination got into the product that was supplied and it was a component in a much bigger and more complex machine, is the supplier liable for the faulty product that was supplied or for the whole machine? The difference can be enormous, as you may imagine.

As far as the supplier is concerned, the last thing it wants to contemplate is those consequent losses. The indemnity will explain what has to happen in such circumstances. There may be, for example, liquidated damages, which is a defined and set percentage of the total value of that part of the order which is under dispute or which caused the problem.

Do be aware of the clauses and their implications and flag them to yourself immediately.

Warranty and Support

This is different from warranties, and will refer to any specific statements, for example that the product will work as designed for at least sixty days. There can easily be trigger words here that you need to recognise, either as supplier or customer.

Support is also important, for obvious reasons, and the terms of the support conditions have to be complied with, as is obvious, but you will need to know how you are either going to receive that support or give it. If there are remote sites, this becomes especially important and this can really be a flash point, especially if the service level agreement (SLA) has been drawn up badly.

For example, it is not unknown for an SLA to state that the supplier must respond within, say, four hours. If the response isn't defined, the supplier may be able to say that merely answering the phone call, phoning back, replying to the email or fax or even acknowledging that there is a problem is a response, and that will easily be possible within the four hours.

This is usually an important area later in contract management.

Risk

This clause will say at what point risk is assumed from the supplier and taken on by the customer. It may have some trigger words and should be carefully understood.

Liabilities of the Supplier and the Customer

This may explain in a different way what the supplier is letting itself in for and what the customer is taking on once the contract is signed. This can be important where there is a further contract entered into by the customer with a third party to supply an order which partly uses the original supplier's products or services. If the customer's supply contract to that third party is terminated unexpectedly, this clause will probably address the outcomes that are envisaged.

Do note that this type of clause can seem very simple at the drafting stage but in real life can be very fraught.

Value Added Tax

Usually boilerplate but this can have interesting implications when dealing with cross-border contracts. There is a magnificently helpful phrase for those who collect VAT which is *deemed supply*, and while this is usually used by revenue agencies to tackle fraudsters, innocent parties can be affected. There is nothing to be done at this point, but just note if there is anything that seems unlikely to be helpful if a dispute arises, by which is meant any statement that says basically it is one side's responsibility if things go wrong with VAT. Such unilateral clauses may not survive legal scrutiny, because they might be deemed unfair, but they can be very costly to resolve.

Third Party Supplier Contracts

These are self-evident as to what they cover, but if any particular third party supplier contracts are mentioned, it will usually be because an issue is anticipated. Take care

Data protection

This is usually boilerplate – and you need to be aware of any data protection considerations, where, for example, you are using your supplier or your customer's database. Note any specific linkage between the contract you are reading and these other contracts. These can be highly contentious when the contract is running in a way that will not have been foreseen all that well in drafting.

Guarantee, Indemnity and Security

This is usually boilerplate, but will impose responsibilities upon the contract manager. The main ones will probably centre on timeliness and that all actions will have to be carried out within a reasonable time frame and to certain ethical standards.

In terms of contract management this is likely to be a flashpoint at some time. If an agreement is needed that something has indeed happened, for example, acceptance of a delivery, and this is not forthcoming in a timely way, it may cause the other party real pain or loss. You will understand this if you are the one waiting for the signed document and any delay will seem unreasonable. On the other side you will be aware of the layers of bureaucracy you have to wade through to get that vital signature and you may think that the elapsed time, in view of what you have to do and the hoops you have to go through to obtain it, is far better than reasonable.

There will, on occasion, be no agreement on this at all and any bad feeling will spill over into other elements of the contract management.

One obvious but often over-looked approach to this potential problem is to ensure that anything you do have actual control over, that doesn't rely on your senior management or the head of sales, is always executed promptly, ahead of expected time, so that you gain a reputation with your opposite number of understanding his or her problems and time scales. When that inevitable slip up occurs, you can point to your track record. It won't solve the problem, but it will mitigate the fall out.

Confidentiality and announcements

Boilerplate and still important because you need to know how formally to send notices and issues to the other side. There will be obligations about confidential information which will need checking just to make sure the clause can be complied with. It is very difficult, for example, to understand where to draw the line between telling a third party enough about a project so that they can help you or supply to you and telling them too much. Sometimes these confidentiality clauses are drawn so tightly it is virtually impossible to say anything.

The answer is to be aware and raise the issue with your opposite number if any such difficulties look like they might arise.

Further assurance

If there are any further assurances, over and above warranties and indemnities, take careful note. They will be in the contract for good reason, even if it is just a lack of trust between the two parties.

Assignment

Boilerplate telling you whether you can or cannot assign part of the contract or whether your supplier can do so. This is rarely a contract management issue.

Whole agreement

Boilerplate saying that the contract constitutes the whole agreement and the other side cannot say that they have some sort of side agreement produced by two senior managers, one from each side, which over-rides the main contract. It may sound absurd but such things have happened and have to be guarded against.

Variation

This is important and although it will likely be boilerplate, it will tell you how, as contract manager, you can approach the other side for a variation in the contract if, for any reason, the sales people, the customer, the lawyers and the senior management who signed the document didn't quite understand how the real world works. For a contract manager this is a vital clause.

Costs

Boilerplate saying that the costs of each side, say, legal fees, will be borne by the side that incurs them.

Notice

Boilerplate saying how you can serve a formal notice on the other side.

Interest on late payment

Standard terms usually, but worth seeing how big the penalty is.

Severance

Severability is a technical term here that means that one rogue clause won't negate the whole contract. For example, if a payment clause has been drawn up in so completely a one-sided way as to be unfair, a court may find that it is unreasonable. Severance states that despite that ruling the rest of the contract is still to be observed.

Agreement survives completion

Boilerplate to cater for, say, confidential information that has been supplied by one side but which will remain confidential after the completion of the contract.

Third party rights

Boilerplate to say that no third parties are involved and that the benefits and liabilities within the contract are solely for the parties to it.

Termination

This has been covered earlier but do be aware of all the likely triggers for termination, not least insolvency of one side or the other, and notice periods. You, as contract manager, are not responsible for the risk involved in termination at will, as that will have been the responsibility of the people who negotiated and signed the contract.

That is the theory.

In practice, if there is a termination at will, the contract manager will be in the firing line, possibly literally. If, for example, the product you are supplying required a huge investment in tooling and that was supposed to be amortised over the life of the contract, but you only have three months in which to terminate the contract, there are going to be some internal issues and the person closest to those internal issues will look the most guilty, even if you had nothing to do with it at all.

Not much you can do about the human nature element of this, but you can be aware and alert people suitably early to the risks, and that might be beneficial.

Assignment

This clause will allow or disallow the supplier or the customer to re-assign the contract to a third party, and explain the terms, if it is allowed.

Arbitration

Instead of going to court to resolve any disputes about the contract, there can be a provision to go to arbitration and or mediation. These are known as alternative dispute resolution or ADR.

The process is like going to court, but it is far less costly and time consuming. This clause, which will probably be mainly boilerplate, will cover a number of issues, including:

- What can go to arbitration
- What triggers arbitration
- Who the potential arbitrator is, usually not an individual but a role

- The terms under which the arbitration decision is made.

The terms will usually insist that the arbitrator's decision is final and there will be an implication that if the arbitrator rules against one party, it will be difficult – it cannot be impossible – to take the dispute to court to have another go.

Clearly arbitration is preferable to litigation in court, but while not so drastic, it is still not a course to contemplate with equanimity as it will still have costs, not least in management time, and it will not be as certain as death and taxes.

The suggestion is that you should understand this clause, if it exists, and you should hold it in mind but only use it as a last but one resort. Whatever else happens you will have lost the relationship by going to arbitration, but even going to arbitration probably says there is no value in the relationship anyway.

Conflicting provisions

Boilerplate explaining what happens if some of the provisions in the contract are in conflict, something that is not unknown. The problem in English law at least is that there is no hierarchy in clauses, so neither the earlier nor the later is more valid. All clauses are of equal standing. You can see why this get out is important.

Successors

Boilerplate to state that if one of the companies is taken over, for example, the terms are still binding on the successors.

Counterparts

Boilerplate which essentially says the parties do not have to get together physically to sign the document but can sign different copies which will be combined, or any other arrangement that allows the signing to be completed without everyone being in the same room at the same time.

Limitation of liability

Boilerplate, mainly focused on rarities like death in service and injury.

Regulatory Issues

Boilerplate that is still important because there will be responsibilities placed on each side and there will be reference to specific regulatory regimes that need to be complied with. Take this as a trigger point and ensure that you understand the implications.

Force Majeure

Usually boilerplate but focused on what happens if something outside the control of either party, such as a hurricane, war, plague, earthquake or political uprising occurs. This isn't usually a high priority for a contract manager and you can hope it doesn't become one.

Governing law and jurisdiction

Boilerplate – but be aware that this can trip people up. Make sure it is the jurisdiction you expect. You won't be able to do anything in particular if it isn't, but you do need to be prepared.

Schedules and Other Appendices

As we mentioned earlier, there will be further elements to the contract, typically after the signing page.

These can include the following headings, with, again, synonyms possible:

- Schedules relating to the contract, such as milestones, delivery dates, and names of specific people associated with the contract
- Service Level Agreements
- Inventories of equipment and other lists
- Warranties and indemnities
- Disclosures
- Statements of work.

There is actually no substitute for working your way through this lot, but again you must take the approach of actively reading them, looking for triggers.

You can see that there are all sorts of traps in these sections of the contract. For example, if there are named people in the contract who are specifically responsible for certain elements, do understand how you can effect changes in this information, because people go off sick, leave the company, are required on more important projects elsewhere, usually explained as family issues, and, or disaffected for some reason beyond your control.

Service level agreements (SLAs) are particularly important and will usually contain triggers words that you should be aware of. Disputes over SLAs can occur over the way the measurements are conducted – when for example did the clock start running against a deadline, was it at the first notification or was it the formal email? Even when the other side complies with the SLA, it can still be a flashpoint as the SLA may cover the actions required at time of signing without actually addressing the main issue. We gave an example above about response times, but if time to repair hasn't been included as part of an SLA, but only time for response, it will be a flashpoint for the contract manager to address.

Inventories are just that, with one word of warning. An inventory is only as good as the day it was written and the person who wrote it. Do establish how the information was verified and whether you have any responsibilities for the equipment being as it is said to be in the list. At some point soon, make a check. If you are responsible for the inventory, that is equipment supplied to you by the other side, this is especially important.

The warranties and indemnities will be the specific statements relating to the earlier clauses covered before. You do need to know these and understand the implications as soon as possible.

Disclosures are statements that one side or the other wishes to make where things aren't quite what they might seem on the surface. These tend to be very specific to the work that is the subject of the contract. A worst case example might be that the supplier is facing litigation over the performance of one or more of the products and wishes to disclose this as a factor in the acceptance of the contract, so that whatever the outcome of the case, this contract is not compromised.

Chapter 6

Managing the Contract

There is a distinction to be made here between project management and contract management. A contract manager may well be the project or programme manager, but the two roles are distinct. Project management is all about ensuring things run smoothly. Contract management has elements of that, but is actually focused on avoiding contractual issues and mitigating them when they arise.

Your role as contract manager is defined by the terms of the contract, and that is why so much time has been spent on reading and understanding the implications of the contract. This book doesn't cover project management proper, but the two roles do dovetail into each other.

Having read and absorbed the contract, which is the fundamental before you can do anything, then comes managing the contract proper.

The standard human response stages applicable to any project usually apply to managing a contract:

- Honeymoon period when the contract is signed and everyone feels happy and not only has no idea what the problems are or likely to be, but what's more couldn't be told and wouldn't believe them anyway
- Disillusionment – when the realisation sets in that the dream that sales sold, procurement shared, senior management welcomed and both sides saw as a win-win contract is actually much more like a nightmare and hardly straightforward
- Practical steps – where the respective contract managers realise that they are saddled with this appalling mistake and have to do something about it (occasionally there is a variation on this where one contract manager tries to place all the burden on the other contract manager)
- Delivery and reconciliation – a long process usually
- Lessons learned – which are actually rarely shared and almost never of any value to the next negotiation.

This cynical view is based on long experience of just such a process, experienced on both sides, and from the perspective of marketing, sales, procurement, negotiations, and contract development and agreement.

It is not possible to circumvent this process, but it is possible to mitigate its worst excesses and this is what contract management is all about.

It is best to have a three point plan at this point and the three points are:

- Communication
- Communication
- Communication.

There really is no other option.

Communication by the contract manager is not however just one way. You need to know what you need to know.

Step 1 – What needs to be communicated to you

The first step is the communication plan, and the first element in that plan is not the normal one of identifying all the things you need to say and all the groups you need to say them to. The first step in your communication plan has to be developing an understanding of all the information you need to have to do your job and who are the responsible people for each aspect of that information and what is the frequency of delivery of that information.

Whether you are the supplier of the buyer you will, for example, need these types of information and an indication of how often it needs to be updated:

- Actual deadlines for documentation, deliveries, people, services and reports
- What contingency is built into any of those deadlines – there will be some
- Availability of products, services, people, equipment, stock, raw supplies, IT systems and IT, data, and reports
- The current position with regard to performance of all elements of the contract, including SLAs, and how often that has to be updated
- Where anything is in the escalation process and why it is there
- Successes
- Outstanding performance by individuals
- Failures.

These all need to be checked back against the triggers and flashpoints that you identified in the reading of the contract. The idea is not to replace the standard project management tools, but to gear everything around the actual contract requirements.

Step 2 – what you need to communicate

You can then create the usual communication plan outline with the headings for what you want to communicate, to whom and how often, and gear it around your needs as a contract manager, but don't create the plan. This communication plan will be a different document from the project communication plan, although they may overlap.

There are two crucial audiences:

- The manager(s) you report to
- Your opposite number.

In fact, the real order is the other way round. Your opposite number will be more important from day one, but as the contract is delivered, the priority will shift a little.

Step 3 – Your Opposite Number

Immediately you have decided to create the communication plan that says what you will communicate and when, but before you create it, go and sit down and work through everything with your opposite number. The actual agenda has to be something like this:

- Reading the contract (good idea physically to do it together tedious though that may sound)
    - Delivery schedules and acceptance criteria
    - Payment terms and processes
    - Triggers
    - Flashpoints
    - Pinch points
    - Dispute resolution processes
    - Concerns and ambiguities
    - Termination clauses
- Immediate issues
- Formal meetings
- Back channels – you will both want this informal route
- Formal reporting
- Informal reporting

- Your prediction of how the various stages associated with any new contract will go.

At this point create the communication plan.

Step 4 – Your Team

Now it is a good idea to assemble your team and share:

- Your triggers and flashpoints in the contract
- The output from your meeting with your opposite number
- Your input needs
- The communication plan
- The contract management issues.

You can then create the plan to manage the contract, again to be shared with the team and in an edited form shared with your opposite number.

Step 5 – Your Management

Depending upon your company you will know the various protocols that you have to observe and what sort of reporting is required and how you need to work with the project or programme manager, if that isn't you. It is probably essential to share with the senior management as much of what you have shared with your team and the opposite number, but you will know what this requires.

The essential element is sharing the pinch points and any flash points that you anticipate and sort out the reporting requirements, and do indicate contractual problems, like conflicting clauses.

Step 6 – Your Contract Management Plan

You have the triggers and flashpoints at your fingertips now, and you need to identify the mitigation that you will employ if any of them arise.

Step 7 – Start Managing the Contract

It will be obvious that managing the contract is different from project management, because you have always got to adhere to the terms and conditions that have been imposed rather than agreeing them with a team as you go along.

Managing the contract is rarely a continuous process, which is why a contract manager may well manage a number of contracts, but it will have intense moments of stress and either side can cause them.

Step 8 – Contingency

This is the step you will hope to avoid and if you don't, you will know that the contract management process has gone awry.

This step is if you have to refer to the contract with your opposite number. Everything that has been discussed so far has been aimed at avoiding going back to the contract with your opposite number but if it becomes necessary do it deliberately and as early as possible.

If it does require such a conversation, and it is probably not a reflection on your contract management although it might be, make it first an informal discussion, the back channel method, and then move to the formal meeting, if that proves necessary, and go through the process of ensuring that every contractual element is considered.

Step 9 – Normal Running

Most of your time as contract manager you will be there to provide legal resolutions to any frustrations caused on either side. You won't be responsible as contract manager for ensuring delivery or acceptance, but you will be there to pick up the pieces where there is a dispute.

The subtitle to this part of the book is certainly ironic. There is no such thing as normal running because it will never feel like that. At every point there will be someone who has misunderstood the contract, failed to deliver, ignored a safeguard, overstepped the mark or just been plain stupid. That is what normal running is as far as the contract manager is concerned.

Chapter 7

Active Reading Summary

When you are reading the contract as part of your preparation for the role as contract manager, and later when the contract is running, remember the aims of active reading, which include paying particular attention to:

- Delivery schedules
- Acceptance criteria
- Payment terms and processes
- Triggers
- Flashpoints
- Pinch points
- Dispute resolution processes
- Concerns and ambiguities
- Termination clauses.

The notes you make about these should be part of your mental furniture at all times as the contract manager.

Chapter 8
The Successful Contract Manager

Without sacrificing your legal position and the fact that you can resort to arbitration if not litigation, your objective as a successful contract manager is to ensure that, as far as possible, the terms of the contract and its focus do not get in the way of a successful project.

This may sound simplistic or common sense, but I have worked with, or actually against, contract managers on the other side who have seen the contract terms as absolutely sacrosanct, even when it is counterproductive to their own company's interests. I can understand why as it is very easy to get sucked into insisting on every element, especially where the project or programme is causing issues. A successful contract manager has to be able to keep all the concerns in mind, understand the detail, but actually always keep in mind the bigger picture.

Your objective as a successful contract manager then is to:

- Avoid disputes and flash points
- Defuse any situations that look as though they may develop into legal conflict
- Mitigate the outcomes of any disputes that you cannot avoid or defuse
- Preserve and strengthen the position of your company under and against the terms of the contract so that if the worst does come to the worst, your position is defensible and reasonable and the company is not exposed to legal challenge of any kind
- Facilitate the delivery of the service and products.

Chapter 9
Reassurance

The one thing that you have going for you as contract manager, despite all the downsides pointed out above, is that from the start both you and your opposite number have a vested interest in making the contract management process effective and in fulfilling the contractual obligations on both sides. Even where it becomes antagonistic, both sides will want to do their best to avoid litigation and even arbitration.

In the heat of the moment it is quite likely that one or both sides will forget this vital fact.

It works for both sides in a contract. For a supplier it is far easier to sell to an existing customer and everything the supplier contract manager does should be informed by this understanding. For a customer, it is far cheaper to procure services from an existing supplier, where you don't have to go through a procurement cycle with all the time it takes, and where you don't have to do such due diligence, and the customer contract manager needs to keep this in mind at all times. Only if the contract breaks down catastrophically should either side contemplate doing other than finding the best way of working together perhaps using all reasonable endeavours, to pick up that point about superlatives.

In order to make contract management work you will need to communicate – listening and getting the information you need first and then explaining to those who need to understand. Earlier in this book, the list of inputs you need was outlined and ensure that you always have timely access to that right information. Explaining and presenting your reports on the status of the project against the contractual commitments is the second part of the communication plan – but still essential.

In short we suggest this acronym, taken with no apology from the financial services industry: KYC.

Know Your Contract but wear your knowledge lightly and only invoke this knowledge when strictly necessary.

Chapter 10
Next Steps

There is no substitute for getting hold of a contract now and starting to understand its structure and then to read it. It is a usual experience to find the first time of reading a contract in such a responsible role rather daunting, but a systematic approach will get you through.

Remember above all the approach to active reading, and make notes about the areas we identified in our advice on active reading.

The way you make notes will depend on your own preferences, but one way is to have an electronic copy of the contract and add your comments to the document as you go through. There are a number of drawbacks to this, one of which is that once you have two copies of a contract, it will be difficult to keep them in synch, as there will be changes over time. The second drawback to this approach is that you then have to plough through the contract looking at the comments each time you are faced with an issue, unless you summarise them as well using the next method.

Experience suggests that it is best to create a different file, either a document or a spreadsheet, in which you tabulate each of the issues as you note them when actively reading the contract.

Chapter 11
Conclusion

Clearly this Bite-Sized Business Book doesn't have all the answers, it may not have all the questions. The objective for the book is to equip you to understand a contract, identify the likely issues and areas that will repay focus, start the process and provide you with a reference for your later actions.

You will no doubt need legal advice at some points where things are not clear, where they are clear but the basis of a dispute, and where there are apparently irreconcilable differences between the parties. You can't rely on this book for such specific advice and the legality of any particular point has to be decided by an expert who knows all the issues and has the legal training

Nevertheless this is a good starting point and is founded on experience over many years of not only negotiating contracts but of managing them. Some of the insights above are the result of painful episodes that the book aims to help you avoid.

BITE-SIZED
BOOKS

Bite-Sized Business Books are designed to provide support and insights for professionals who are tackling an unfamiliar task either for the first time or after a gap, as well as those who want to find new ways of doing what they are familiar with.

They are deliberately short, easy to read, step-by-step books guiding the reader through the various stages behind each business process or activity, with a clear focus on outcomes. They are firmly based on personal experience and success.

The most successful people all share an ability to focus on what really matters, keeping things simple and understandable. MBAs, metrics and methodologies have their place, but when we are faced with a new challenge most of us need quick guidance on what matters most, from people who have been there before and who can show us where to start. As Stephen Covey famously said, "The main thing is to keep the main thing, the main thing".

But what exactly is the main thing?

Bite-Sized books were conceived to help answer precisely that question crisply and fast and, of course, be engaging to read, written by people who are experienced and successful in their field.

The brief? Distil the "main things" into a book that can be read by an intelligent non-expert comfortably in around 60 minutes. Make sure the book enables the reader with specific tools, ideas and plenty of examples drawn from real life and business. Be a virtual mentor.

Bite-Sized Books don't cover every eventuality, but they are written from the heart by successful people who are happy to share their experience with you and give you the benefit of their success.

We have avoided jargon – or explained it where we have used it as a shorthand – and made few assumptions about the reader, except that they are in business, are literate and numerate, and that they can adapt and use what we suggest to suit their own, individual purposes. Whether you are working for a multi-national corporation or a start-up or something in between, the principles we introduce will hold good.

They can be read straight through at one easy sitting and then used as a support while you are working on what you need to do.

Bite-Sized Books Catalogue

Business Books

Ian Benn
>Write to Win
>>How to Produce Winning Proposals and RFP Responses

Matthew T Brown
>Understand Your Organisation
>>An Introduction to Enterprise Architecture Modelling

David Cotton
>Rethinking Leadership
>>Collaborative Leadership for Millennials and Beyond

Richard Cribb
>IT Outsourcing: 11 Short Steps to Success
>>An Insider's View

Phil Davies
>How to Survive and Thrive as a Project Manager
>>The Guide for Successful Project Managers

Paul Davies
>Developing a Business Case
>>Making a Persuasive Argument out of Your Numbers

Paul Davies
>Developing a Business Plan
>>Making a Persuasive Case for Your Business

Paul Davies
    Contract Management for Non-Specialists
Paul Davies
    Developing Personal Effectiveness in Business
Paul Davies
    A More Effective Sales Team
        Sales Management Focused on Sales People
Tim Emmett
    Bid for Success
        Building the Right Strategy and Team
Nigel Greenwood
    Why You Should Welcome Customer Complaints
        And What to Do About Them
Nigel Greenwood
    Six Things that All Customer Want
        A Practical Guide to Delivering Simply Brilliant
        Customer Service
Ian Hucker
    Risk Management in IT Outsourcing
        9 Short Steps to Success
Marcus Lopes and Carlos Ponce
    Retail Wars
        May the Mobile be with You
Maiqi Ma
    Win with China
        Acclimatisation for Mutual Success Doing Business
        with China
Elena Mihajloska
    Bridging the Virtual Gap
        Building Unity and Trust in Remote Teams
Rob Morley
    Agile in Business
        A Guide for Company Leadership
Gillian Perry
    Managing the People Side of Change
        Ten Short Steps to Success in IT Outsourcing

Saibal Sen
>   Next Generation Service Management
>   > An Analytics Driven Approach

Don Sharp
>   Nothing Happens Until You Sell Something
>   > A Personal View of Selling Techniques

Lifestyle Books

Anna Corthout
>   Alive Again
>   > My Journey to Recovery

Phil Davies
>   Don't Worry Be Happy
>   > A Personal Journey

Phil Davies
>   Feel the Fear and Pack Anyway
>   > Around the World in 284 Days

Regina Kerschbaumer
>   Yoga Coffee and a Glass of Wine
>   > A Yoga Journey

Arthur Worrell
>   A Grandfather's Story
>   > Arthur Worrell's War

Public Affairs Books

Eben Black
>   Lies Lunch and Lobbying
>   > PR, Public Affairs and Political Engagement – A Guide

Christian Wolmar
>   Wolmar for London
>   > Creating a Grassroots Campaign in a Digital Age

Made in the USA
Las Vegas, NV
18 November 2023

81127113R00022